AMAZING SUMMER OLYMPICS

GYMNASTICS

BY MARI BOLTE

CREATIVE EDUCATION • CREATIVE PAPERBACKS

Published by Creative Education and Creative Paperbacks
P.O. Box 227, Mankato, Minnesota 56002
Creative Education and Creative Paperbacks are imprints of
The Creative Company
www.thecreativecompany.us

Design by The Design Lab
Production by Alison Derry
Art direction by Tom Morgan
Edited by Alissa Thielges

Photographs by Alamy (PA Images), Getty (BSR Agency, Central Press, Gerlach Delissen – Corbis, Jamie Squire, Laurence Griffiths, Patrick Smith, Picture Alliance, Tim Clayton – Corbis), Shutterstock (Image Source Collection)

Copyright © 2024 Creative Education, Creative Paperbacks
International copyright reserved in all countries. No part of this book may be reproduced in any form without written permission from the publisher.

Library of Congress Cataloging-in-Publication Data
Names: Bolte, Mari, author.
Title: Gymnastics / by Mari Bolte.
Description: [Mankato, Minnesota] : [Creative Education], [2024] | Series: Amazing Summer Olympics | Includes bibliographical references and index. | Audience: Ages 6–9 years | Audience: Grades 2–3 | Summary: "Celebrate the Summer Olympic Games with this elementary-level introduction to the sport of gymnastics and its floor and apparatus events. Includes biographical facts about Hmong-American artistic gymnast Suni Lee"— Provided by publisher.
Identifiers: LCCN 2023007973 (print) | LCCN 2023007974 (ebook) | ISBN 9781640267657 (library binding) | ISBN 9781682773154 (paperback) | ISBN 9781640009356 (pdf)
Subjects: LCSH: Gymnastics—Juvenile literature. | Artistic gymnastics—Juvenile literature. | Gymnastics for women—Juvenile literature. | Summer Olympics—Juvenile literature. | Lee, Sunisa, 2003–Juvenile literature.
Classification: LCC GV461.3 .B65 2024 (print) | LCC GV461.3 (ebook) | DDC 796.44—dc23/eng/20230322
LC record available at https://lccn.loc.gov/2023007973
LC ebook record available at https://lccn.loc.gov/2023007974

Printed in China

Table of Contents

Gymnastics Beginnings	4
Routines and Disciplines	7
Artistic Gymnastics	11
Rhythmic Gymnastics	15
Trampoline	16
Incredible Athletes	19
Competitor Spotlight: Sunisa Lee	22
Read More	24
Websites	24
Index	24

Female gymnasts performed at the 1908 Olympics but could not compete.

In ancient Greece, people exercised in places called gymnasiums. They were places to strengthen the body and the mind. The first modern Olympic games in 1896 had **artistic gymnastics**. Women's gymnastics was added in 1928.

artistic gymnastics a form of gymnastics where competitors perform short routines while using special equipment

5

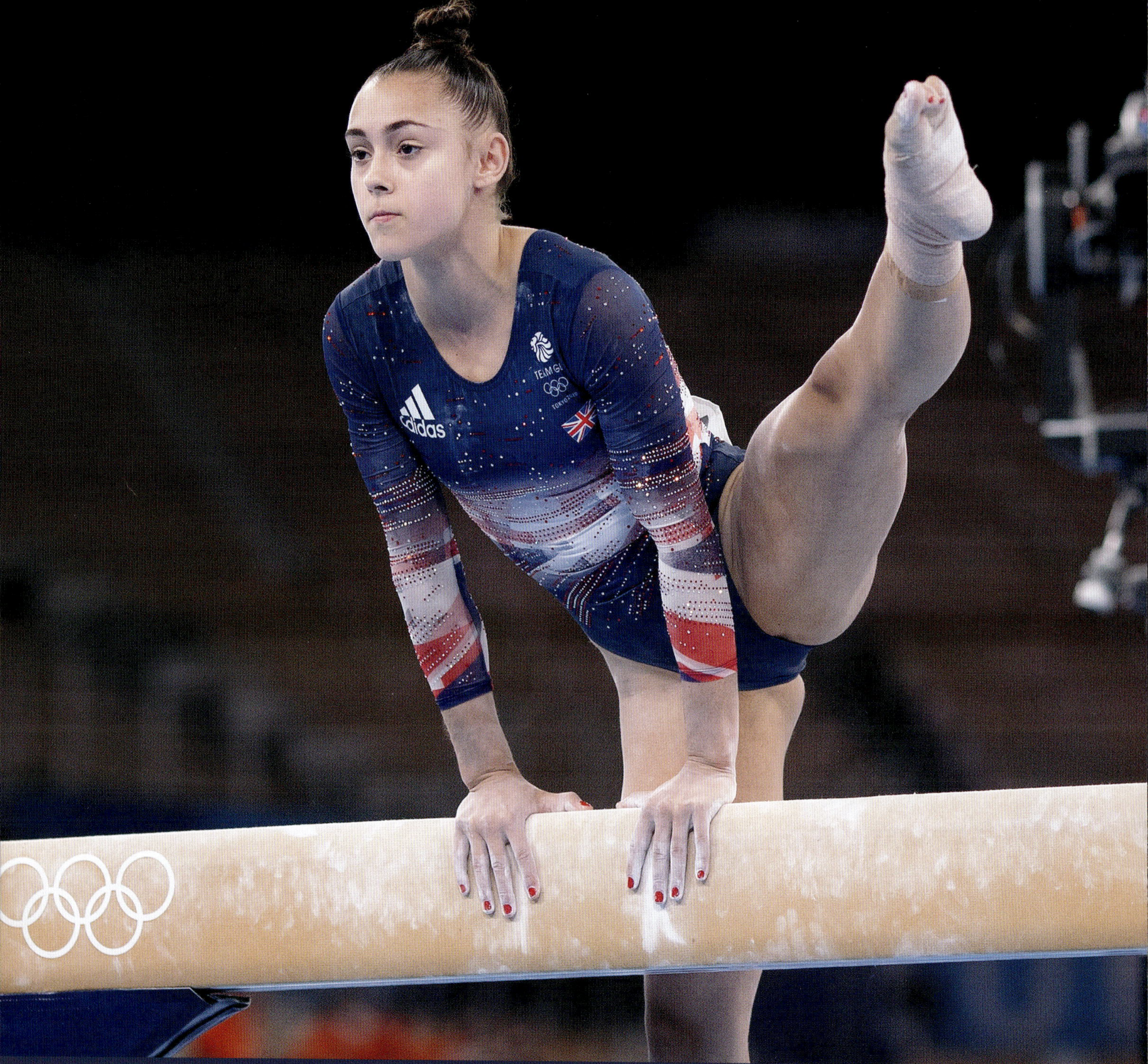
adidas
TEAM GB

Routines are fast and intense, with movements done one after the other.

Gymnasts perform exercises called routines. They show off their strength, balance, and **flexibility**. Each routine is judged. More difficult movements are worth more points. Points are taken away for mistakes or falls. Scores are usually close. A tenth of a point can make a difference.

flexibility the body's ability to stretch and bend

The rings event takes incredible upper body strength.

Gymnastics has three forms, or disciplines. They are artistic, trampoline, and rhythmic. Both men and women compete in artistic and trampoline. Only women compete in rhythmic. Men have more artistic events.

Women gymnasts perform their floor routines to music. Men do not.

9

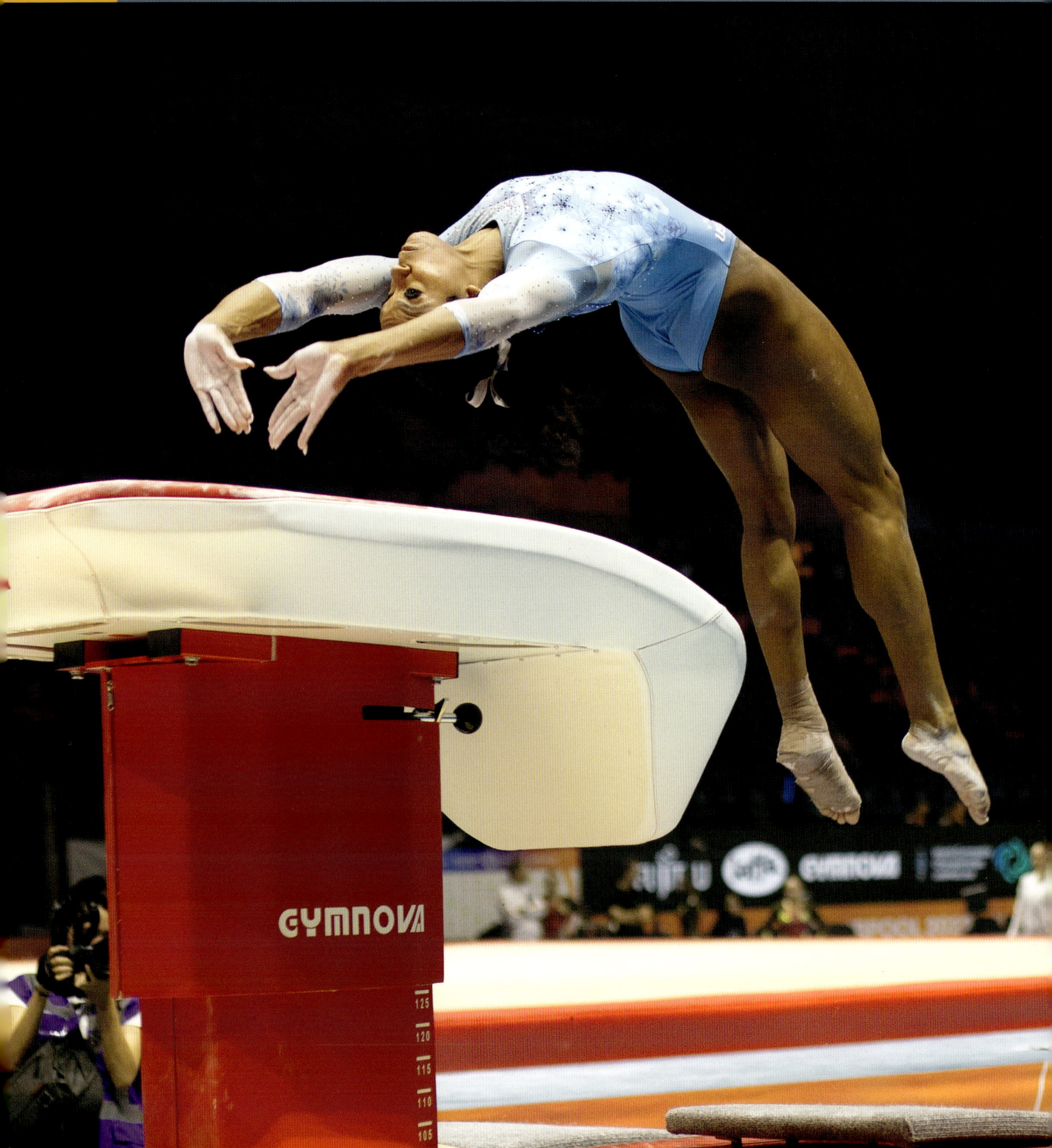
GYMNOVA

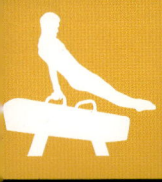

Vault is scored the same for men's and women's events.

Women gymnasts compete in four artistic events. They are floor exercise, uneven bars, **vault**, and balance beam. Men also compete in floor and vault. Pommel horse, rings, parallel bars, and horizontal bar are the men's events. There are team and individual events. Gymnasts can also win **all-around**.

all-around an event where a gymnast's individual scores are combined to determine a winner

vault an event where gymnasts launch off a springboard with their hands to do flips

Twelve men's teams and 12 women's teams compete in artistic. Another 50 men and 50 women can compete individually. Gymnasts must make it through rounds of tests first. Winners of these qualifying rounds go to the event finals.

Judges score a routine's difficulty and how well the gymnast did the moves.

13

GYMNASTICS

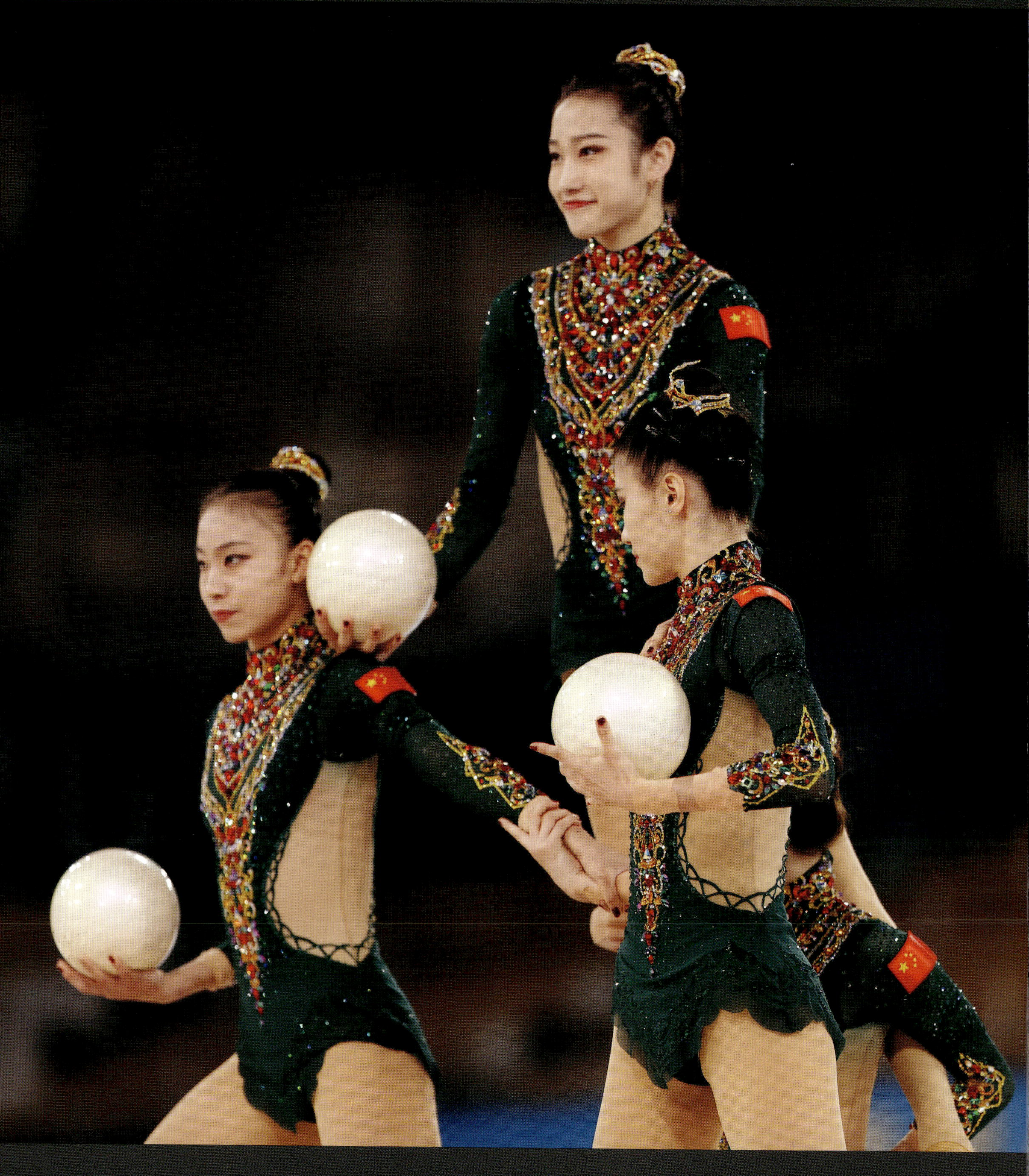

Rhythmic gymnastics was added to the Olympics in 1984. It combines dance and artistic moves. There are team and individual events. Gymnasts use props like hoops, ribbons, balls, and clubs. Their routines are set to music.

In team events, balls may be thrown and bounced as part of the routine.

Trampoline joined the Olympics in 2000. Men and women both have an event. They must show 10 skills while jumping between 2 trampolines. Each skill is given a point value. Gymnasts are also judged on how long each skill takes.

Large mats catch gymnasts if they fall off the trampoline.

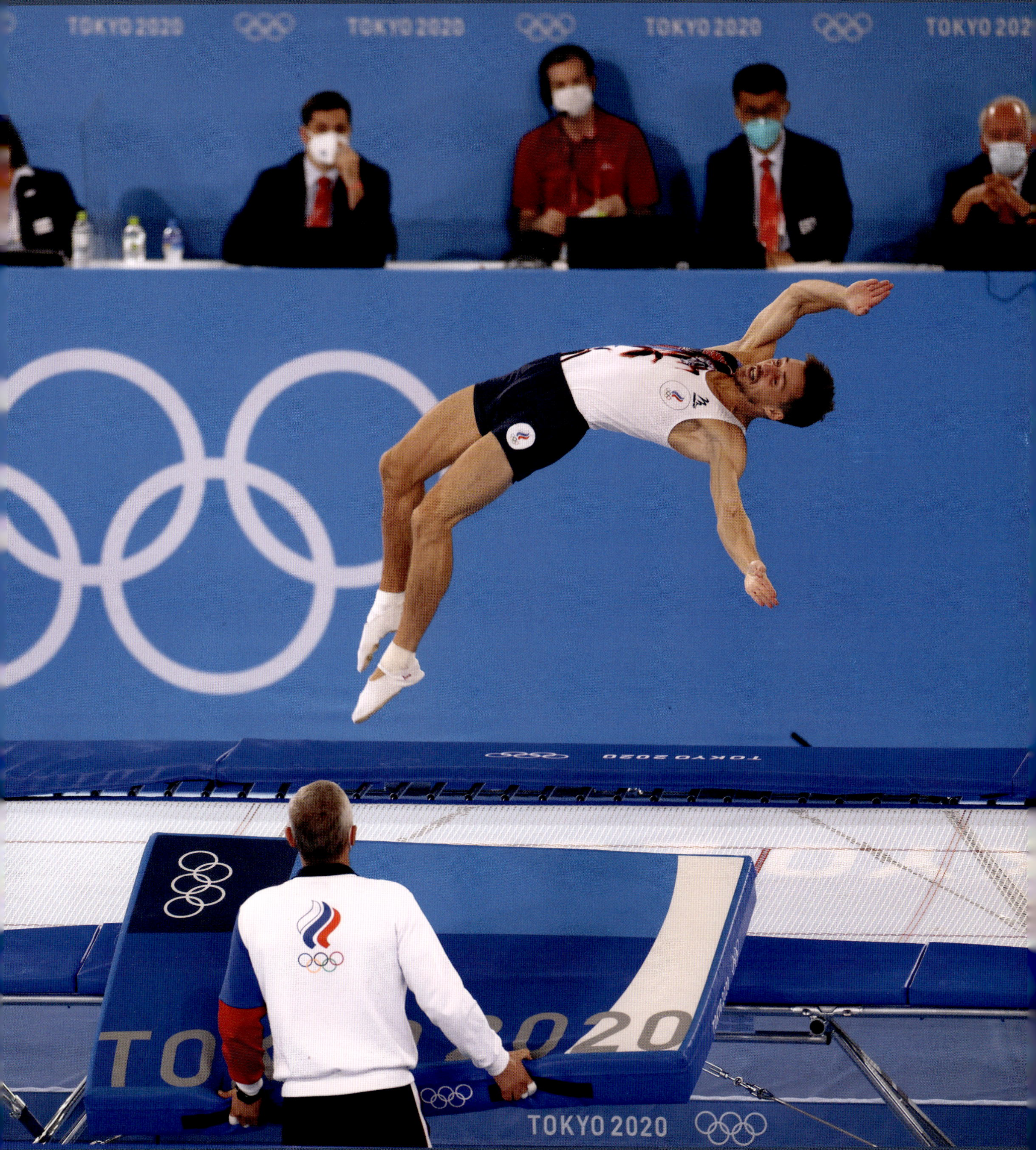
TOKYO 2020
TOKYO 2020
TOKYO 2020
TOKYO 2020
TOKYO 2020

GYMNASTICS

Simone Biles competed in the team vault and individual balance beam at Tokyo 2020.

Simone Biles is the most decorated U.S. women's gymnast ever. She has won seven Olympic medals. Biles has four **signature moves** named after her.

signature move a move awarded to the first gymnast to successfully perform it in competition

Chalk keeps hands from sticking, helping gymnasts swing easily around the bar.

Gymnasts fly through the air. They do backflips across beams. They lift their bodies using their incredible arm and core strength. Don't miss these athletes at the next Summer Olympic Games!

The best gymnasts make the sport look effortless.

21

Competitor Spotlight: Sunisa Lee

Sunisa "Suni" Lee lives in St. Paul, Minnesota. She competes in artistic gymnastics. Her first Olympics was Tokyo 2020. She took home the bronze medal in uneven bars. Her routine was the most difficult in the world. Lee also earned the all-around gold medal. Lee was the first Hmong-American to represent the United States in the Olympics.

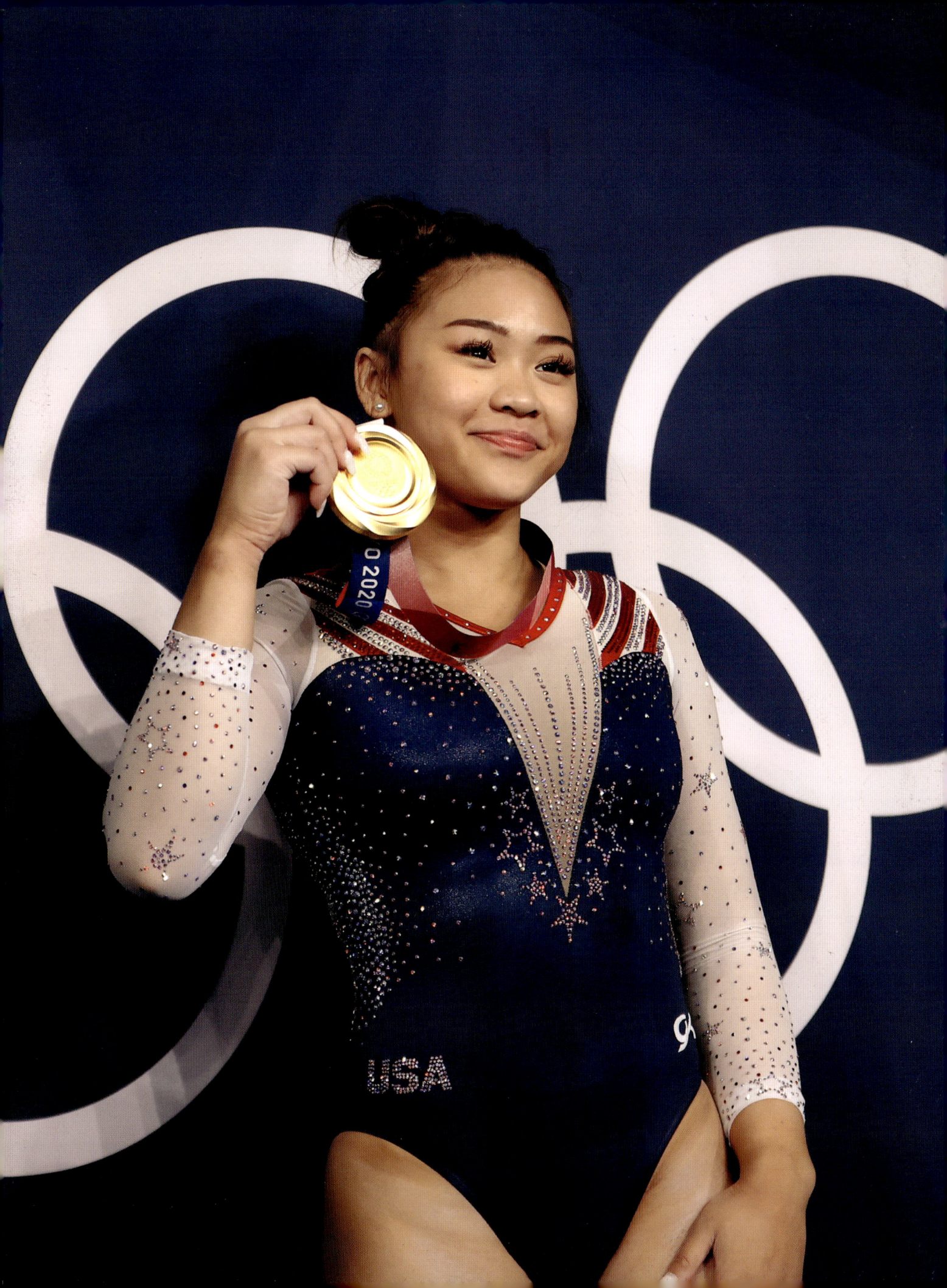

Read More

Cox Cannons, Helen. *What You Never Knew about Simone Biles.* North Mankato, Minn.: Capstone Press, 2023.

Forsberg, Jennie. *Rhythmic Gymnastics.* Minneapolis: Abdo Kids, 2023.

Lawrence, Blythe. *Trailblazing Women in Gymnastics.* Chicago: Norwood House Press, 2023.

Websites

Artistic Gymnastics
https://olympics.com/en/sports/artistic-gymnastics/
Read about gymnastics' Olympic history and current athletes.

DK Find Out: Gymnastics
https://www.dkfindout.com/us/sports/gymnastics/
Learn fun facts about gymnastics.

Note: Every effort has been made to ensure that the websites listed above are suitable for children, that they have educational value, and that they contain no inappropriate material. However, because of the nature of the Internet, it is impossible to guarantee that these sites will remain active indefinitely or that their contents will not be altered.

Index

artistic, 4, 8, 11, 12, 22
Biles, Simone, 19
history, 4
Lee, Sunisa, 22
men's events, 8, 11, 16
rhythmic, 8, 15
routines, 7, 8, 12, 15, 22
scoring, 7, 11, 12, 16
team events, 11, 12, 15
trampoline, 8, 16
women's events, 4, 8, 11, 16